contents

introduction

You will soon be celebrating your child's first Holy Communion. There is excitement in the air. It's a very special event.

As a parent you share in your child's happiness. But you may also feel a little unsure. You may have a personal anxiety or be confused about changes in the way first Holy Communion is now celebrated. If you are not a Catholic you may understandably feel concerned about such a Catholic event as your child's first Holy Communion.

We hope this book will dispel any anxieties and help you to prepare for and enjoy the occasion. It is not a religious instruction book, nor a rule book. It is simply a clear and straightforward guide for all parents whose children are making their first Holy Communion.

The most important point to remember is that this is a time of happiness and celebration for you and your child. It is a day of thanksgiving to God for having brought you this far as a family, and a confident prayer for your child's future, which is safe in God's hands.

Sammy was tired. The family had been out all day and he didn't want the day to end. "Stay with me," he begged his mother. But his mother was only too well aware of all she had to do before her own bedtime. "I can't stay any longer," she replied "but when I'm gone, just cuddle your teddy very tightly and you won't feel lonely." Sammy wasn't going to be so easily quietened, "When I'm lonely, a teddy bear's no good to me. I need someone with skin on their face!"

All these signs of love and commitment help us to sense the touch of the Creator in our world. But God was not content with just that. He sent us an even more eloquent sign: his Son, Jesus Christ. Jesus Christ is God "with skin on his face" — Jesus is God made flesh. In his healing, forgiving and preaching, Christ showed us how close God is to each one of us.

Christ left his Church to continue his work of revealing God's closeness to the world. The Church (that is the community of Christ's followers, not the buildings) is called to be a living, human sign of his continuing presence in the world today.

A child's sleepy reply points us to a fundamental need in all of us to have a sign of a living presence with us. We need signs of life because signs of life are signs of hope, pointing to a future and to new experience.

The miracle of life is all around us. We feel instinctively the mystery of creation, the mystery of love, in a way words cannot express. The touch of a hand, a fleeting glance, a certain smile between people in love, can speak more eloquently than any words. In the same way, a solitary tear can reveal unspeakable pain or sadness.

As Christians, our unity with Christ is maintained and strengthened at special moments. We call these special moments "sacraments". When we celebrate a sacrament we draw close to Christ by recalling his life and actions. At these times we experience the love of our heavenly Father through ordinary human events: being born into a family, sharing a meal, being healed and forgiven.

Just as a shared glance between lovers is a sign of intimacy which words cannot describe, so the sacraments are a sign of our intimate union with God. They are God's way of saying "I love you".

your child's first

communion

- What does your child need to know?

- Inside a seven-year-old's mind

- What happens on the day?

acknowledgments

Design: The Stream, 01252 810033

Photography: John Crone and library images

Published by:

REDEMPTORIST PUBLICATIONS

Copyright © 1990 Redemptorist Publications

First Published: May 1990

Redesigned: September 2005

Nihil Obstat: Cyril Murtagh, V.G. Censor Deputatus

Imprimatur: +Crispian Hollis, Episcopus Portus Magni

Portus Magni May 1990

The Nihil Obstat and Imprimatur are a declaration that a book or pamphlet is considered to be free from doctrinal or moral error. It is not implied that those who have granted the Nihil Obstat and Imprimatur agree with the contents, opinions and statements expressed.

ISBN 0 85231 311 X

All rights reserved. No part of this publication may be reproduced, stored in a retrieval system, or transmitted in any form or by any means, electronic, mechanical, photocopying, recording or otherwise, without prior permission from Redemptorist Publications.

Printed by iprint Leicester LE8 6ZG

Redemptorist
PUBLICATIONS
Chawton Hampshire GU34 3HQ
Tel: 01420 88222 Fax: 01420 88805
www.rpbooks.co.uk
rp@rpbooks.co.uk
A Registered Charity

Jesus once walked the streets of Palestine, and people could see him, hear him and touch him. His healing love, his compassion, his forgiveness were made tangible. In the special events we call sacraments we believe that Jesus is still present to us in a way that we can see and hear and touch. In the sacraments we meet him as God "with skin on his face".

Seven signs of life among Christians

1. Baptism
2. Confirmation
3. Eucharist

These are the signs that we have become Christians and joined the family of God. They are called the sacraments of initiation. Baptism and Confirmation are signs of our birth as Christians and can never be repeated. The Eucharist – or Mass – is the continual celebration of Christian life.

4. Marriage
5. Holy Orders

Marriage is the sign that a man and a woman have vowed to belong exclusively to each other in a permanent partnership of mutual love and care. It is a sacrament which provides the basis for the birth of children and the development of family life.

In the sacrament of Holy Orders members of the Christian community are ordained to share in a special way in the priesthood of Christ. The priest is the teacher and leader of the community.

6. Reconciliation
7. Anointing

As we go through life as Christians we fall sick either physically, mentally or spiritually. We need healing and a chance to begin again. These are the signs which remind us of God's continuing love and forgiveness towards us. They are the sacraments of healing which maintain Christians.

why Mass and Holy Communion are important to Catholics

"Marriage to a Catholic, while an experience to be recommended, does entail far more than might be expected from the pre-sales talk. It is one thing to marry a single loved one; it is difficult to appreciate that you also marry into a large family and a complete parish. In many cases the sheer scale is overwhelming. On its own, the family is a great source of joy, and every significant event in life is an excuse for a party — fair enough — but also for yet another Mass. The frequency of these is daunting as, for me, time stands still during Mass. My feelings cannot be appreciated for inevitably at least one kindly soul will ask 'Wasn't that a lovely Mass?' What am I supposed to reply? I wouldn't know where to begin!" *Chris*

Chris expresses clearly the feelings of many people who are married to Catholics. There is often confusion and misunderstanding about what the Mass means and why it is so important to Catholics. And Catholics themselves are not always very good at explaining it. To an onlooker, it might seem that what happens at Mass bears little or no relation to what's going on in the world. The Mass is then seen as boring and irrelevant.

Catholics see it differently. We believe that what happens at Mass is really a picture of what is happening in the world. We believe that the Mass is like a lens which brings into sharp focus a lot of things which we often completely overlook. Through this lens we can see the true nature and meaning of our world and the reason for our existence. By looking at what happens at Mass we begin to see the world in a new way. So let's look a little more closely at the Mass.

Coming together

The first thing you will notice is people coming together. They come from different homes and different situations: some happy, some sad, some fulfiled, some lonely. But there is a unity. Catholics are united in that they think that coming together for

Mass is important. This is because they believe that, despite all the problems, God's power is at work in the world and God's strength can overcome human weakness. Catholics believe that this is true for people of every race, colour and creed.

Our coming together as Christ's followers brings this belief in God's power within each one of us into focus.

Listening

The second thing you will notice at Mass is that very soon everyone sits down to listen to the scriptures being read. There are lots of ways in which we believe that God has spoken and continues to speak to people. Human experience and our own conscience, for example, are ways in which God touches everyone. Yet for Christians there is something more: Jesus Christ and all that he taught us about God and his love for his people. That's why at the final reading, which is from the Gospels, we stand to listen to the words Jesus himself spoke.

When we listen to God's word in the scriptures it brings God's voice in the world into focus.

Thanksgiving

The third thing you will notice as central to the Mass is what Catholics call the Eucharistic Prayer. The word

Eucharist comes from the Greek word meaning "thanksgiving". Everyone gathers around the altar with the priest to re-enact what Christ did with his disciples at the Last Supper. We listen afresh to Christ's words thanking and praising God saying,

"Take this, all of you, and eat it: this is my body which will be given up for you."

Then,

"Take this, all of you, and drink from it:
this is the cup of my blood,
the blood of the new and everlasting covenant.
It will be shed for you and for all
so that sins may be forgiven.
Do this in memory of me."

We believe what Christ said. We believe that when we remember and act on his words, Jesus is present. This is the most precious moment of life. The bread and wine which have been brought forward to represent our life and work, are now changed into the Body and Blood of Jesus Christ. He is present, as he said he would be, and is our reminder of God's unending promise. But this precious moment doesn't mean that what's happening in the rest of the world is irrelevant. The opposite is true. This moment reminds us of the importance of every single person in God's eyes.

Our celebration of Christ's presence among us brings into focus just how precious is the whole of God's world.

Communion

Finally, at the heart of the Mass, is Holy Communion. This is a personal moment. When we share in this sacred meal we do indeed share in the life of Christ.

We are experiencing the result of God's great desire to come to us and be one with us. To make the bread and wine for our Communion, grapes and grain are crushed. Jesus Christ was also crushed for our Communion. He was crushed and crucified on the cross, so that the power of God's love for all could be shown. In all our lives there is suffering, but our suffering is not meaningless. For when suffering is faced with love, that which was crushed and broken is transformed by such love into new life.

Our celebration of Communion brings into focus the cost of all true loving and shows us where such love will lead us — into the hands of God the Creator of love.

The first but not the last

Catholics can sometimes overlook the fact that the power of Christ does not weaken as we grow older. Although our first Holy Communion is a very special event for all those involved, its benefits are not "once and for all". We must continually overcome our inclination to sin and selfishness which separate us from God. That is why our first Holy Communion should be just that: the first of many more as long as we live. For whenever we come together for the Mass, Christ comes among us reassuring us of his love and refocusing our view of the world.

inside a seven-year-old's mind

Usually, Catholic children make their first Holy Communion around the age of seven. As you prepare your child to receive the sacrament it can be helpful to understand what makes a seven-year-old tick. Children do not all develop at the same pace, of course. But the attitudes, values and ways of thinking of the average seven-year-old are very different from those of an adult. The following guidelines will help you to understand your child's outlook on the world and prevent you from expecting too much too soon.

• Seven-year-olds are eager to belong. They want to be accepted and recognised as part of the family or community. They have a strong desire to conform and therefore they imitate the actions, attitudes and values of their parents.

• They have a strong desire to please their parents and they see right and wrong very much in terms of the rules their parents lay down for them. Something is "wrong" if it displeases Mummy or Daddy.

• They have little notion of personality or inner feelings. They define themselves and others by their actions and by the group they belong to. They are very loyal to their friends.

• Their ability to think in abstract terms is very limited. So words like salvation, faith, hope, redemption, forgiveness, grace, and so on, mean very little to them.

• Their religious sense is strong. They have a deep sense of awe and wonder at the world around them. They are curious about God and about death and may well ask questions about them.

• The faith of seven-year-olds relies heavily on the stories, rules and values of the family and community to which they belong. They attach great importance to knowing and conforming to these.

parents matter most

"Your child wants you to assist him in using his own resources and to recognise and be proud of his accomplishments. Your support will give him the impetus to carry on."

Dr Lee Salk

"The blame for parental ineffectiveness often rests with the child psychiatrists, psychologists, teachers, social workers, and paediatricians like myself. In the twentieth century parents have been persuaded that these are the only persons who know for sure how their children should be managed.

This is a cruel deprivation that we professionals have imposed on mothers and fathers. Of course we did it with the best intentions. We didn't realise, until it was too late, how our know-it-all attitude was undermining their self-assurance as parents."

Dr Benjamin Spock

"You start by loving. Loving a child won't solve all the problems, but unless she is loved, nothing else will ever help enough."

Joan Beck

"The presence and availability of fathers to children is critical to their knowledge of social reality, their ability to relate to male figures, to their self-concepts, their acceptance of their own sexuality, their feeling of security."

Henry Biller

"If you truly love and respect your child, you can make certain mistakes and it won't be the end of the relationship. You don't have to be a perfect parent, because the underlying foundation is there."

Herbert Kohl

You know your child best and you know the kind of home environment you have created. How can you develop the introduction to Christ, which you have already made at your child's Baptism, in ways that are right for you and your family?

For a variety of reasons, you may not have been very active in the practice of your faith in recent years, so you may want to spend some time thinking about this. Try to decide where you want to go from here in your own life of faith. Think through your hopes and beliefs about life, death, your faith and your family. Try to focus on what God means to you personally despite any unhappy experiences you may have had with individual Church members or your own religious upbringing.

Once you have thought about your own hopes and expectations about faith and the place of God in your life, try to do the same exercise in relation to the life of your family. How can you build a sound faithstyle within your home, based on Christ's pattern for his followers?

what does your child need to know?

There are many excellent programmes available for the preparation of children for their first Holy Communion. The programme your parish follows will provide plenty of lively and interesting material for your child and may supply some background information for you too.

Parents are not expected to exercise the skills of a trained teacher of religion. In fact, the contribution of parents to the development of their children's faith is much more profound.

All first Holy Communion programmes recognise the central place of parents in their child's religious development. Your contribution is irreplaceable.

Your child needs to know that he or she is unique

Every child is special, with individual gifts, talents and potential. There has never before been a human being quite like your child and there never will be again. Each person is a one-off creation, and therefore of priceless value. Make sure that your child knows this and make sure that he or she knows that this is how you view every other person too. This is important because it is only in this way that a child can begin to understand the significance of creation and the value of all God-given life.

Your child needs to know that he or she is loved permanently and unconditionally

Your child needs to know this when they are good, bad, attractive, unattractive, clean, dirty, at home or away. Make sure that you tell your child how precious they are to you and how much you love them. Try to create an atmosphere of love in your home which is unconditional and which includes everyone you share your lives with, including yourself. This means that even when your child or someone else does

something wrong, lets you down or behaves badly, you can make it clear that you reject and dislike the behaviour but not the person, not your child. This is important because it is only through the experience of unconditional love that a child can begin to understand God's love for us.

Your child needs to know that other people are also unique, valuable and lovable

You have let your child know that he or she is unique and lovable and so are all other people regardless of race, creed, colour, class or age. Here your influence is vital. Parents can provide a sound foundation for young children to learn and experience freedom from prejudice. It is in the relationships you form, and the kind of family life that you create, that your child will learn your values and attitudes towards others. It is in this setting also that the foundations of a child's concept of loving acceptance and forgiveness are laid.

Your child needs to know that God is at the heart of creation

As you tell your child about life, the world around you and your relationships, talk also about the influence of God, as you see it, in all of these areas. Talk about how you see God, what you find easy about being a Christian and what is not so easy. If you are not a Christian yourself, it is helpful to tell your child this and also to talk about your commitment to your Christian partner. In this way your child learns about tolerance, understanding and commitment.

Your child needs to know the stories of the Gospels

Talk or read about the life of Christ: the kind of person he was, the stories he told, the way he treated people. Explain that Jesus was the Son of God who came to show us how to live a life of love. Don't feel you have to offer a complete course of Bible study. Simply make your child familiar with the Gospel stories and with Jesus Christ.

Your child needs to know how to communicate with other people

Try to make sure that you create times in the day when you can talk to one another and listen to one another as a family. Whether your family consists of just you and your child or you are part of a larger group, make sure you give full attention to everyone. Mealtimes provide a good opportunity for communication. If that is not a daily custom in your home, try to share a morning cup of tea, coffee or a bedtime drink, when you can talk a little and share what is going on in your lives. If that doesn't work in your family try to find things you can do together which will give you an opportunity to share yourselves with each other. We need to plan such times, otherwise the days slip by and we find we really haven't communicated for ages.

Your child needs to know how to pray

The only way we can learn to pray is by doing it. Make prayer a part of your everyday family life. It doesn't have to be a long drawn-out affair. Nor do you need special books, special words, special positions or special facial expressions! Simply choose a few moments, perhaps your child's bedtime, and sit together thanking God for the day. Say sorry to one another and to God for things that have gone wrong, remember anyone who may be

sick or having a difficult time, and ask God's blessing on one another. If you don't pray together at present, don't worry. The fact that your child is preparing to celebrate his or her first Holy Communion provides you with an ideal reason for introducing prayer into your family. Let your child know that you pray. There's no need to make a big fuss about it. Simply make it clear that you pray about any problems or difficulties that arise and that you thank God for his blessings. Think about going to Mass regularly if you don't go often; perhaps try going during the week sometimes. Make sure, though, that you don't start trying to force all your family to pray whether or not they wish to. That is one way of making sure that they never pray! By helping your child to become familiar and comfortable with prayer, you will help him or her to begin to build a deep and very personal relationship with God.

What the Church requires

Children must be baptised and it is required that they have sufficient knowledge and careful preparation to understand the mystery of Christ according to their capacity, and can receive the Body of the Lord with faith and devotion. Children should also have the opportunity, after appropriate preparation, to receive the Sacrament of Reconciliation before making their first Holy Communion.

1 There seems to be a great emphasis on Catholic family life in the preparation programme my child is following. My partner is not a Catholic. How can I avoid him feeling left out?

You are right to be sensitive about not allowing your partner to feel excluded. Although there may be a number of Catholic practices which your partner will not be at home with, the essential elements in any child's upbringing are love, security and a feeling of self-worth. It is in these most important areas that you and your partner can work together. As a Catholic you will have some special experiences to share with your child. Undoubtedly your partner, too, has a number of unique gifts. If you recognise and acknowledge these gifts your partner will know that he is not excluded.

2 I am not a Catholic and all the hype surrounding first Holy Communion seems rather excessive and has little to do with God. Can't they cut down on some of this fuss?

It's understandable that people who are not Catholics sometimes find the activities surrounding the celebration of first Holy Communion rather strange. It has to be admitted that the behaviour of some Catholics doesn't help. Some seem to place all the emphasis on the clothes, photographs, and an amazing amount of often sugary, cheap-looking religious articles and accessories, frequently accompanied by emotional outbursts. Often the more distant the Catholic is from the practice of their faith the greater the importance placed on such aspects of first Holy Communion. The true meaning and significance of a wedding can often get lost in superficiality and the same is true of first Holy Communion. The true meaning and significance as outlined in this book, however, remains authentic.

3 We have been asked to attend a parents' group but with shift work and long hours we can't manage it. Will this affect our child?

Parents' groups are often organised in order to help parents feel part of the preparation of their child. They are not compulsory. Explain to the organiser that you are unable to attend and ask for details of the contents of the course so that you can follow what your child is doing and can then talk together about it. Let your child know that you are interested and want to be involved. Try, too, to make sure you have complete details about the practical timetable and arrangements for the day itself.

4 In our parish, preparation for first Holy Communion is all organised by the priest's favoured few. Why should I have to dance to their tune?

Preparation for first Holy Communion used to be very much in the hands of the Catholic school. Home and parish were often excluded. The result could be an imbalance. Today there is a realistic attempt at partnership, recognising that each area of a child's life has an important part to play in religious formation. The religious education class is concerned with deepening your child's religious knowledge. Your home is the place where your child grows daily in faith, and the parish is where everyone comes together to celebrate their faith. As you can see, the part you have to play is of equal value and importance to the others.

5 I am divorced and remarried in a civil ceremony so cannot go to Holy Communion. What can I do on the day?

This is a common problem for a number of Catholic parents, so don't feel you are alone. But although it is so common the reasons and the history of each relationship vary so much that it is impossible to give general guidance for all. Make an appointment in good time to discuss this with your parish priest or with a priest with whom you can talk comfortably. Don't be afraid of being absolutely honest about your situation and he will help you to arrive at the answer that is right for you.

6 I am a single parent, living with my partner. What can I do on the day?

You can do exactly the same as every other parent present; enjoy the day. Try to ensure that your child also enjoys the day and is beginning to understand what it means to be a Christian. If you are unable to receive Holy Communion yourself, choose a suitable opportunity before the day and take time to explain to your child that you are unable to receive Holy Communion because of your present situation. Children are amazingly understanding and sympathetic about such matters and the fact that you are present and taking part and celebrating, will be the most important point for your child.

7 My child attends the Catholic school but I have not practised my faith for years. What should I do?

When your child was baptised you undertook to bring your baby up as a Christian. Clearly, you have begun to honour that promise in ensuring that your child is receiving a Christian education. There can be many reasons why someone ceases to practise their faith. Perhaps now is the time to try to think through your own values and attitudes. What are the things that really matter to you? Answering that question can help you clarify the kind of religious upbringing you want for your child, regardless of past experiences. Pray for guidance and try to find someone you can talk to about your faith or lack of it. It will make an important difference to your child if you are clear about your own faith at this stage in your family life.

8 My child is a stepchild. The preparation programme asks lots of questions about family history. Will everyone get to know our personal business?

This is a common and growing anxiety for many parents. Some years ago when the present forms of sacramental preparation programmes were being developed, those responsible were anxious to base a child's blossoming awareness of God on the lived experience of the child. In their enthusiasm for this they sometimes overlooked the reality of many family situations. The result was that all too often children were asked seemingly innocent questions about where they were born? Who was around then? What does mum do? What does daddy do? Can you bring a photograph of that time? etc. The problem with such questions is they are innocent unless you don't fit into that pattern; then they become a nightmare and an unacceptable intrusion.

Today, there is a much greater awareness of the need for more sensitivity in such areas and parents are quite justified in refusing to take part in any programme which infringes on the privacy of their family life for any reason. Any parish supporting a programme which is too intrusive should reconsider its value.

9 My child attends a local-authority special school. Parish preparation doesn't cater appropriately, but I don't want my child to be left out of yet one more part of parish life. Where do I go from here?

Go and see your priest or the head teacher at the local Catholic school. They will be able to suggest what would be best for your child. There are a number of special programmes available for sacramental preparation and many areas have a skilled teacher locally who can offer the right kind of preparation for individual children.

10 My son is nearly eleven and so much older than the other children making their first Holy Communion. What can I do?

Your son doesn't have to prepare for his first Holy Communion with the others and it is quite usual for a child to make first Holy Communion individually. It's best to see your parish priest who will be happy to make special arrangements. However, he will want to be confident that you will offer your child plenty of support, especially by going to Mass with him regularly.

the catechist

Catechist is a funny word. It's not likely that you will run into it at the checkout in the supermarket or on the garage forecourt. It is part of the language of the Church. And because we don't hear it very often it tends to have a certain mystique about it: a catechist must be something special, an expert or a very holy person even.

In fact, all the word catechist means is one who teaches by word of mouth — the word comes from the Greek, katecheein, which is to din into the ears! So a catechist is simply one who has the ability to teach Christianity in the most basic way — by word of mouth. Of course, today, most catechists use a number of ways to teach the faith: drawings, videos, music and storytelling. Often a parish catechist is a teacher or a religious sister, but increasingly more laypeople from all kinds of backgrounds are becoming involved in the work.

In many parishes a team of catechists is responsible for the formal religious education of all the children from five to sixteen. For the first Holy Communion group, the catechist will usually follow a specially designed programme, planned to cover all your child needs to know at this stage. One thing catechists cannot do, and indeed should never even attempt to do, is to eclipse or contradict what is taught at home about Christian living. All formal teaching in the parish should complement the teaching that parents offer in terms of experience, shared living and example.

Usually there will be at least one meeting for parents during your child's instruction, and it is important that you try to attend in order to be familiar with what your child is being taught. It also means that you can ensure that there are no conflicting areas between home and class.

The catechist, like yourself, will be anxious to do what is best for your child and will appreciate any insights you can give. If there is anything you are worried about or would like clarified don't feel shy about asking questions. And feel free to contact the parish priest directly if there are any personal matters relating to your child's celebration of first Holy Communion which you prefer to keep confidential.

questions children ask and how to answer them

Children can ask very difficult questions and find the most awkward moments to ask them. Don't worry if you can't answer their questions easily. Be honest and say so. Often your child will be happy to have posed the problem and may not want a particularly detailed answer. Nonetheless, it will help if you have some idea how to approach the questions children commonly ask.

How can Jesus look like bread and wine?

When Jesus was on earth he looked just like us. He had a body like ours. Now Jesus has a different kind of body because he rose from the dead and is so powerful that he can be everywhere. He is with us in a very special way in Holy Communion because he wanted to make it easy for us to know that he is with us and is close to us.

How does Jesus get into the host?

We believe that the host becomes the body of Jesus when the priest says the words of Jesus, "This is my body, given for you". We don't know how it happens but we believe it because Jesus tells us it is so. We know that it is possible because Jesus showed the power of his words at another time when he fed the crowd of five thousand people with just five loaves and two fishes.

Why do we go to Mass?

We go to Mass for several reasons. The first is to thank God for all that he has done for us. We also go to join with our friends, family and other Christians in praising God and listening to his word. Most important of all, we go to Mass to become one with Jesus in receiving him in Holy Communion as he asked us to do.

Why doesn't Mummy go to Communion?

Because Mummy is a Catholic there are certain rules which she tries to keep. At present she's not able to keep some of them and so she doesn't feel that she can receive Holy Communion when she goes to Mass.

Why isn't Daddy a Catholic?

People get to know God in lots of different ways. The way each person gets to know God often depends on what country we live in and where we grew up. These differences are important because they affect the way people live. Daddy is not a Catholic but he and I share our lives and respect each other's beliefs.

Why aren't my prayers answered?

It might not seem like it but prayers are always answered. We may not get the answer we want but our prayers will be answered. When you ask for something, I have to think whether it is a good idea or not. I have to decide what is best. I don't love you any less when I say "No". God, too, is full of love for you and always gives you what is best even if you can't see it at the time.

Will I feel different after Holy Communion?

Special events can often make us feel excited or nervous, and that may be how you feel on the day of your first Holy Communion. Receiving Holy Communion has to do with our faith not our digestion, so you will not feel any sudden physical difference, neither will you be changed instantly into an angel or a saint. But you will know that Jesus has come to you in a special way, helping you to become a better and more loving Christian.

special needs

Some children, do not fit into the usual patterns of preparation for first Holy Communion.

It may be that your family has moved frequently and your child has missed the preparations for first Holy Communion. There is no specific age for this sacrament and there is no reason why your child should not make their first Holy Communion at a time when you feel it is appropriate. There is also no reason why you should not prepare your child yourself for this sacrament. Your parish catechist or priest will be able to suggest suitable material.

Sometimes a child may have missed school as a result of illness or may have some learning difficulties which mean that his or her reading ability is at a different level from the rest of the group. Preparing for first Holy Communion has nothing to do with our reading skills and there need be no reason why your child should not be prepared using alternative methods and materials.

Children who are handicapped, either mentally or physically, will have special needs in their religious education.

Sometimes this results in isolation from the rest of the children in the parish. It is important that this is avoided as much as possible.

Physically handicapped children may simply need facilities which enable them to join in with the rest of the group. If there are no such provisions don't be reluctant to ask why they are absent.

If your child is mentally handicapped, you may feel unsure about the right time to begin preparation for first Holy Communion. Most dioceses now have a special centre which advises on religious education for children with handicaps. Find out your local office and ask for someone to call to see you. There are some useful sacramental preparation programmes available, specially designed for children with mental handicaps.

It is important for children to feel that they belong, that they are part of their peer group. It follows then, that the celebration of first Holy Communion should incorporate all the children within a parish. Even if the preparation has to be done individually there should be some attempt to do things together wherever possible.

*Photo thanks to
the Treloar Trust*

make it a memorable occasion

First Holy Communion is probably the most important personal religious event that your child will remember. The right atmosphere and the right memories are vitally important. Keep that in mind during all your preparations.

• Talk with your child about the hopes and plans for the day. Tell your son or daughter about your own first Holy Communion. What was important then? What didn't matter but seemed important at the time? Talk about what went wrong, what went right, about what's happened since then, and perhaps any regrets you have. Ask any other children in the family to do the same.

• Ask your child to share with you their hopes and fears for their first Holy Communion day. What is important to them and what doesn't matter so much? Make sure you touch on practicalities and ordinary aspects, not just "holy" matters! Discuss plans for preparations for the day and how you will deal with them together.

• Ask the catechist in good time what the local custom is about the way the children are dressed for their first Holy Communion in your parish. You will then have time to ensure that your child isn't anxious about how they will look on the day. Try to avoid making too much fuss about the outfit, or it will begin to seem as though the clothes are the most important part of the day. Don't feel you have to spend a lot of money on clothes. Keep it simple.

• Initiate some special prayertime — even if you have never done so before, perhaps at bedtime or

just after teatime. Avoid anything too heavy and long-winded, centre it on your child to begin with.

• Use this opportunity of the celebration of first Holy Communion to talk to your partner about faith, your lifestyle, your plans and your own relationship and future.

• Reflect on how you can live as a Christian family. Try introducing some simple practices about your commitment to the community: such as offering an elderly person a lift to Mass on a regular basis or offering to help with a parish activity. Think about the way you use your money, your time, your gifts and perhaps the way you treat one another.

• Talk to your child about why you chose their baptismal name. Perhaps talk about their patron saint if you can find out about them.

• Think about ways of creating a lively environment of living Christianity in your home which is realistic, practical and tolerant. Make a resolution to ensure that you include a sense of humour and fun as well as a sense of awe before God. (Christians sometimes forget that there are 81 references in the New Testament reminding us of Christ's instructions to be joyful.)

• Make plans in good time for celebrating the day. What would your child like, what would you like, what would your partner like? What's the local custom? How can you combine all four? (This is where you may find you need some of that sense of Christian humour referred to in the previous section.) Try to make at least one meal a week a special event at which you come together as a family. This provides an opportunity to talk, share what's happening in your lives and reinforce your commitment to one another as a family.

• Don't force your non-Catholic partner into taking a more active part than they may wish to in the celebration. And don't allow yourself to be forced into taking part in anything you are unhappy about.

• If there is anything concerning the preparation that you are unhappy or worried about, do tell the catechist, teacher or priest.

• Take time out to relax together as a family. Fix a time right now!

• Most important of all – assure your child of your genuine interest in all the plans, preparations and events on the day and especially – now and always – your interest in and commitment to your child.

what happens on the day?

Each parish makes its own plans for the celebration of first Holy Communion. Often the details will depend on whether or not the school is involved, whether the celebration takes place at the main parish Mass or whether it is a separate event. In some parishes the children who are making their first Holy Communion are all seated together at the front of the church. In other churches children are encouraged to sit with their families.

Whatever the plans in your parish check the following points:

• Make sure you are familiar with the local arrangements and the reasons for them. Then, if any of your family raise questions about it, you know the answers.

• If you are unhappy about any of the arrangements speak to the catechist or the parish priest in plenty of time before the big day.

• Before insisting on any change based on personal preference think through the effect on your child if they are made to feel the odd one out.

• Try to make sure that your child is carrying as little as possible. Cluttered hands can make receiving Holy Communion a nightmare on such a special day.

• Make sure your child knows where the nearest toilets are so that there need be no crisis if they are excited or nervous on the day.

• If you or your partner are worried about receiving or not receiving Holy Communion yourselves on the day, make an appointment to see your parish priest in plenty of time before the event, so that you need have no last minute anxieties which may affect your child.

• Try to relax and enjoy the celebration yourself. See it as a milestone in your child's life of faith and a fresh phase in your own Christian life as a mature adult.

• Remember: first Holy Communion is not an end but a beginning.

Heavenly Father, make me a better parent.

Teach me to understand my children, to listen patiently to what they have to say, and to answer all their questions kindly.

Keep me from interrupting or contradicting them.

Make me as courteous to them as I would have them be to me.

May I never laugh at their mistakes, or resort to ridicule when they displease me.

Bless me with the confidence to grant them all their reasonable requests and the courage to deny them privileges I know will do them harm.

May I not rob them of the opportunity to think, to choose and to make decisions for themselves.

Make me fair and just and kind.

And fit me, O Lord, to be loved and respected and imitated by my children.

Cary C. Myers

Redemptorist
PUBLICATIONS

ISBN 0-85231-311-X

9 780852 313114